Sanjeev Kapoor's

TV DINNERS

Published by
POPULAR PRAKASHAN PVT. LTD.
301, Mahalaxmi Chambers
22, Bhulabhai Desai Road
Mumbai - 400 026
for Khana Khazana Publications Pvt. Ltd.

First Published 2009
First Reprint 2014

(4151)
ISBN 978-81-7991-403-8

Design: Quadrant Infotech (India) Pvt. Ltd.
Photography: Bharat Bhirangi
Food Stylist: Anupa Das

PRINTED IN INDIA
by Infinity Advertising Services Pvt. Ltd.
D – 4/2, Okhla Industrial Area Phase-1
New Delhi 110020

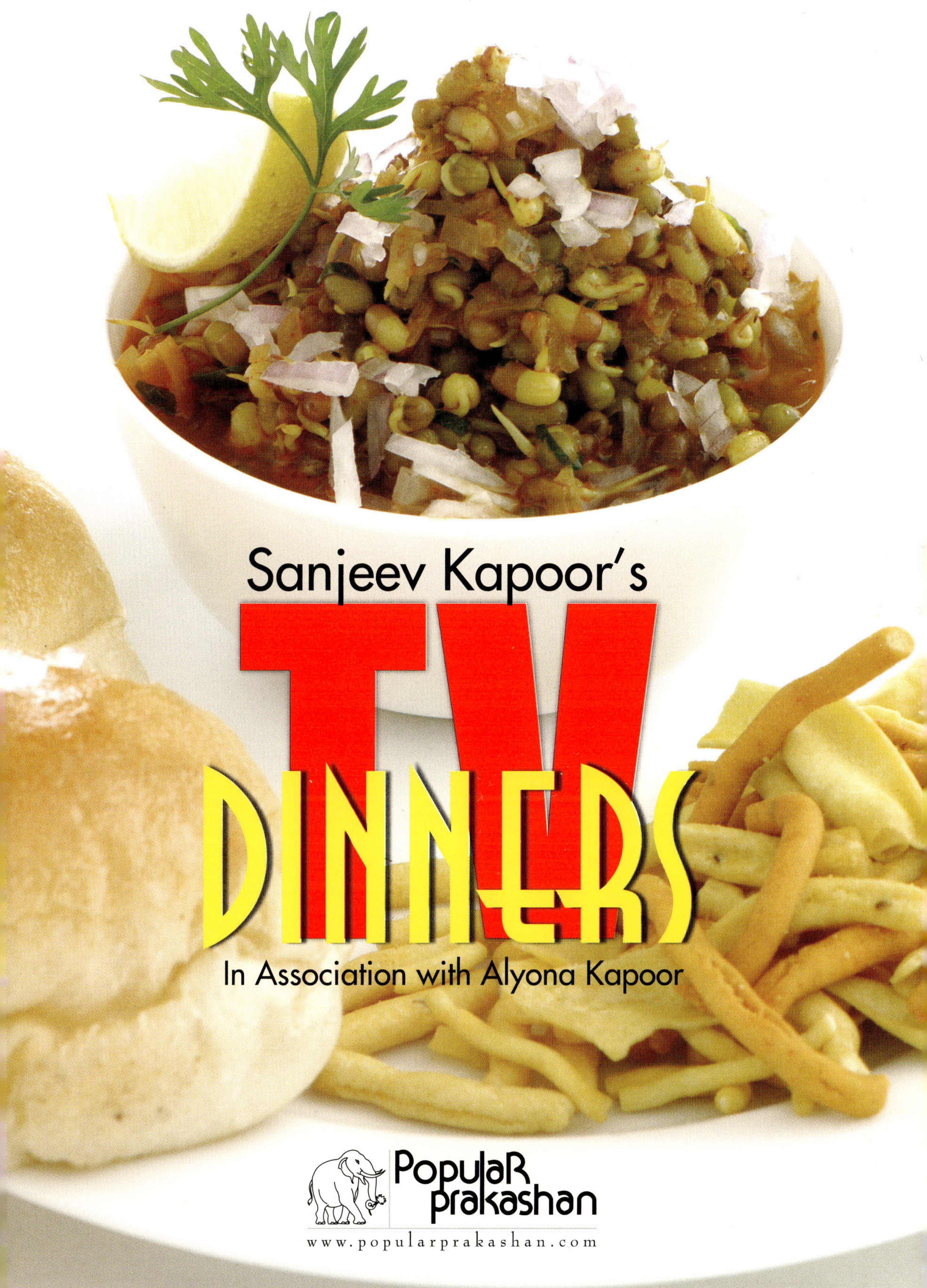

Sanjeev Kapoor's

TV DINNERS

In Association with Alyona Kapoor

Popular Prakashan

www.popularprakashan.com

AUTHOR'S NOTE

The only thing constant in life is change! My latest offering, TV Dinners, is all about change… changing the food habits, particularly of those who love eating in front of the telly! What really happens when we eat while watching TV? I can think of three things: we do not look at the food much, we do not taste the food much but we do eat too much! I have invariably found that we tend to overeat while watching TV. Those who understand the term 'couch potatoes' will agree!

So my take on this is, why not divert some attention from the TV and that remote control in your hand towards the food in your plate? Is it what you like? Is it nutritious? Is it comforting? Is it tasty?

My collection of recipes that qualify for TV dinners is proof that one-dish meals can be balanced, tasty and novel too. TV Dinners in the West are usually frozen dinners, microwaveable meals or ready-to-eat meals. They are pre-packaged, frozen or chilled meals which usually come in individual portions. They require very little preparation and contain all the elements for a single serving. Though the concept is around fifty years old, its popularity continues, but with many evolutionary changes. For example, the aluminium tray that needed to be heated in an oven has now been replaced with a food tray made of microwaveable material, usually plastic. You will also find meals labelled 'gourmet', 'organic', 'vegan' or 'kiddy meals'; but the fact remains that these meals are not freshly made. The freezing process tends to ruin the taste of food, and the meals are usually heavily processed with extra salt and fat to compensate.

AUTHOR'S NOTE

A TV dinner, in my definition, would mean anything that is nutritious, and that can be served and handled easily. Plus it is filling enough to do away with the craving for snacks that are devoid of nutrition. I am not suggesting that munchies be banned; but the quantity consumed can be drastically cut down. The need of the hour is to remove all junk food from our diets!

So a TV Dinner could mean a slightly westernised *Bread Salad with Diced Chicken* or a *chatpata* snack like *Black Grape Pani Puri*. It could mean a wholesome *Missal Pav* or a creamy *Risotto Primavera*. You could combine these with sweet somethings like *Sticky Date Pudding* or *Vanilla Sponge with Fruit Cream* and then dump all the dishes in the sink to be washed the following morning if the movie is really very good!

Stack up your favourite programmes, stock up on your favourite ingredients and cook up some delights that enhance the joys of watching TV!

Happy Viewing!

Contents

8 Shaami Kabab Wraps

10 Baked Bean Wraps

12 Black Grape Pani Puri

14 Vegetable Triple-Decker Sandwich

16 Barley and Crunchy Nut Salad

18 Warm Thai Noodles and Papaya Salad

21 Bread Salad with Diced Chicken

23 Chicken and Spinach Pizzas

24 Minestrone Toscano with Pesto Croûte

26 Sweetcorn Soup with Mixed Vegetables and Tofu

28 Pav Bhaji Roll-Ups

30 Penne in Thousand Island Dressing

32 Cheesy Macaroni

34 Chicken and Spinach Bake

37 Spaghetti with Chicken and Pesto

39 Baked Mixed Vegetables

40 Chilli-Lemon Stewed Noodles with Vegetables

42 Dal Dhokli

44 Frittata with Caramelised Onions and Roasted Peppers

46 Hariyali Tikki with Chole

48 Wholesome Spaghetti

50 Tacos with Refried Beans, Salsa and Crispy Vegetables

53 Tex-Mex Pasta

55 Stir-Fried Medley

Contents

56 Quick Jeera Chicken

58 Shanghai Stewed Noodles

60 Soya Granule Lasagne

62 Spinach and Cheese Pie

64 Missal Pav

66 Multi-Grain Foot-Long with Mushrooms and Chicken Salami

69 Oodles of Noodles

71 Paella with Tofu

72 Brown Rice Biryani with Chutney Chicken

74 Cheesy Rice-Stuffed Peppers

76 Chicken Stew with Garlic Bread

78 Corn and Coriander Rice

80 Erra Saadam

82 Goan Fish Curry with Red Rice

85 Jammu ka Aloo-Anardana Parantha

87 Kesari Seafood Pulao

88 Mushroom Pot Rice

90 Risotto Primavera

92 Saoji Mutton

94 Vanilla Sponge with Fruit Cream

96 Sticky Date Pudding

98 Green Chutney, Thousand Island Dressing, Chicken Stock and Vegetable Stock

99 Mayonnaise and White Sauce

SHAAMI KABAB WRAPS

Roti as a kabab holder works well for the avid TV watcher! No mess, no clean-ups!

Ingredients

600 grams boneless mutton, cut into 2-inch cubes
½ cup split Bengal gram (*chana dal*), soaked
2 medium onions, chopped
2 tablespoons chopped fresh coriander (*hara dhania*)
2 tablespoons chopped fresh mint (*pudina*)
2 teaspoons lemon juice
2 tablespoons oil +, for shallow frying
½ teaspoon cumin seeds (*jeera*)
1 teaspoon coriander seeds (*dhania*)
5-6 black peppercorns (*kali mirch*)
3-4 black cardamoms (*badi elaichi*)
2 inches ginger, chopped
10-12 garlic cloves, chopped
1 teaspoon red chilli powder
1 teaspoon *garam masala* powder
½ teaspoon mace (*javitri*) and green cardamom (*chhoti elaichi*) powder
Salt to taste

To serve

8 large wholewheat (*atta*) *rotis*
8 tablespoons Green Chutney (page 98)
8 lettuce leaves
1 large onion, sliced
1 teaspoon *chaat masala*

Method

1. Mix together the chopped onions, coriander and mint with the lemon juice to make a stuffing. Divide into sixteen portions and set aside.
2. Heat two tablespoons of oil in a pressure cooker; add the cumin seeds, coriander seeds, peppercorns and black cardamoms and sauté for half a minute over a moderate heat. Add the ginger, garlic and chilli powder.
3. Add the boneless mutton and *chana dal*. Add two cups of water and bring to a boil. Seal with the lid and cook under pressure for about twenty-five minutes till the pressure is released six times (six whistles).
4. Remove the lid when the pressure has reduced completely. Cook over a high heat till the mixture is fully dry, stirring continuously.
5. Remove from heat and set aside to cool. Grind the mutton and *chana dal* mixture to a smooth paste. Add the *garam masala* powder, mace and cardamom powder and salt. Mix well and check the seasoning.
6. Divide the mixture into sixteen portions. Flatten each portion in the palm of your hand and place a portion of onion stuffing in the centre. Shape into round patties and flatten slightly.
7. Heat the oil in a frying pan and shallow-fry the *kababs* till golden brown. Drain on absorbent paper.
8. Spread some green chutney on each *roti*. Tear a few lettuce leaves and place over the chutney. Place two *kababs* on each *roti*. Sprinkle onion slices and *chaat masala*. Roll up, wrap in aluminium foil and serve immediately.

BAKED BEAN WRAPS

Different from the usual baked beans on toast, easy to make and serve, baked bean wraps will earn you a lot of appreciation!

Ingredients

4 wholewheat *rotis*
1½ cups tinned baked beans
2 medium onions
1 tablespoon oil
1 medium green capsicum (*hari Shimla mirch*), chopped
5-6 garlic cloves, thinly sliced
3 tablespoons chopped fresh coriander (*hara dhania*)
Tomato ketchup, as required
Red chilli sauce, as required
A few iceberg lettuce leaves, shredded
4 tablespoons grated processed cheese

Method

1. Finely chop one onion and slice the other.
2. Heat the oil in a pan; add the chopped onion, capsicum and garlic, and sauté for a few minutes.
3. Add the baked beans and sauté for a while. Add the chopped coriander and mix.
4. Place the *rotis* on a flat surface. Spread a little tomato ketchup and red chilli sauce on each one.
5. Place some of the baked bean mixture at one end of each *roti*. Sprinkle the sliced onion, lettuce and grated cheese over the baked beans and roll up.
6. Cut each roll into diagonal pieces and serve; or wrap each roll in aluminium foil and serve.

BLACK GRAPE PANI PURI

This pani puri is so easy to make and so delicious that it will constantly be in demand!

Ingredients

Crisp *puris* (meant for *pani puri*), as required
1 litre fresh black grape juice
½ medium bunch (100 grams) fresh mint (*pudina*)
¼ medium bunch (100 grams) fresh coriander (*hara dhania*)
3-4 green chillies
2 tablespoons tamarind (*imli*) pulp
Salt to taste
½ teaspoon black salt (*kala namak*)
1 teaspoon roasted cumin (*bhuna jeera*) powder
1 teaspoon red chilli powder
1 tablespoon lemon juice

Filling (optional)

Sprouted green gram (*ankurit moong*), as required
Potatoes, boiled and mashed, as required

Method

1. Grind the mint, coriander and green chillies to a fine paste.
2. Mix together the black grape juice, ground paste, tamarind pulp, salt, black salt, roasted cumin powder, chilli powder and lemon juice.
3. Chill in the refrigerator till required.
4. To serve, place a little sprouted green gram or mashed potato in each *puri*, fill with the grape juice mixture and eat at once.

VEGETABLE TRIPLE-DECKER SANDWICH

Stacked up and filling: perfect with a masala movie!

Ingredients

8 slices brown bread
4 slices white bread
3 medium potatoes, boiled and grated
Salt to taste
20 black peppercorns (*kali mirch*), crushed
1 teaspoon red chilli flakes
1 medium green capsicum (*hari Shimla mirch*), chopped
2 tablespoons cheese spread
2 medium onions, cut into round slices, rings separated
2 medium cucumbers, sliced
2 medium tomatoes, sliced
5-6 pickled gherkins, sliced vertically
2 tablespoons butter

Method

1. Place the potatoes in a bowl. Add salt, half the crushed peppercorns, the chilli flakes, capsicum and cheese spread and mix well.
2. Use one slice of white bread and two slices of brown bread per sandwich. Butter the slices lightly on one side.
3. Spread the potato mixture evenly on one slice of brown bread. Place some onion rings, sprinkle a little salt and a little crushed peppercorn and cover with a slice of white bread. Place a few cucumber and tomato slices on the bread. Sprinkle salt. Place a few gherkin slices and cover with the second slice of brown bread and press down lightly.
4. Heat a sandwich grill. Spread butter over the top slice and place on the hot grill and press down with the top of the grill.
5. Once the grill marks are seen, remove, cut into triangles and serve hot.

BARLEY AND CRUNCHY NUT SALAD

Soft barley pearls are a perfect contrast to crunchy peanuts and cucumbers. The celery gives the salad a nice fresh taste.

Ingredients

1 cup barley (*jau*)
½ cup peanuts (*moongphali*), roasted
Salt to taste
2 large cucumbers, seeded and cut into small pieces
2 large tomatoes, seeded and cut into small pieces
2-inch celery stalk, chopped
2 tablespoons chopped fresh coriander (*hara dhania*)
5-6 black peppercorns (*kali mirch*), crushed
2 teaspoons lemon juice
4 large lettuce leaves

Method

1. Soak the barley in three cups of water for six hours. Drain and pressure-cook with three cups of water and salt till almost done. Drain and set aside to cool.
2. In a large bowl, combine the barley, peanuts, cucumbers, tomatoes, celery, chopped coriander, salt, crushed peppercorns and lemon juice and toss well to mix.
3. Arrange the lettuce leaves on a serving platter, spoon the tossed salad onto the bed of lettuce and serve immediately.

WARM THAI NOODLE AND PAPAYA SALAD

Add this exotic dish to your TV dinner list...

Ingredients

100 grams cellophane or glass noodles
½ medium unripe green papaya, sliced
3 tablespoons oil
4 garlic cloves, chopped
½ medium green capsicum (*hari Shimla mirch*), cut into ½-inch pieces
1 celery stalk, sliced
2 tablespoons fish sauce (optional)
Salt to taste
¼ teaspoon white pepper powder
½ cup roasted peanuts (*bhuni moongphali*), crushed
1 cup bean sprouts
1 tablespoon lemon juice
1 tablespoon chopped fresh coriander (*hara dhania*)

Method

1. Soak the noodles in hot water for a few minutes. Drain and refresh in cold water. Add one tablespoon of oil and toss to coat the noodles with the oil.
2. Heat the remaining oil in a pan. Add the garlic and stir-fry for a few minutes or until light golden brown. Add the papaya slices, capsicum and celery and stir-fry for a minute.
3. Add the noodles and toss. Season with the fish sauce, salt and white pepper powder. Remove from heat.
4. Add the crushed peanuts and bean sprouts. Add the lemon juice, mix well and serve warm, garnished with the chopped coriander.

BREAD SALAD WITH DICED CHICKEN

Tired of the usual chicken and bread combo in a sandwich? Serve them up as a salad!

Ingredients

3-inch piece of French loaf (*baguette*), cut into small cubes
2 (200 grams each) boneless chicken breasts, boiled and cut into small cubes
6 tablespoons olive oil
1 tablespoon vinegar (*sirka*)
2-3 garlic cloves, chopped
½ cup fresh basil (*tulsi ke patte*) + a few to garnish
Salt to taste
2 medium tomatoes, seeded and cut into small pieces
1 large cucumber, seeded and cut into small pieces
4 lettuce leaves

Method

1. Preheat the oven to 180°C/350°F/Gas Mark 4.
2. Scatter the bread cubes in a shallow baking dish and toast in the preheated oven for ten minutes, or till crisp and golden brown. Remove from the oven and set aside to cool.
3. Combine the olive oil, vinegar, garlic, basil and salt in a food processor and blend at high speed for a few seconds to make a coarse paste. Transfer the paste to a large bowl.
4. Add the toasted bread cubes, chicken, tomatoes and cucumber and toss well. Let the salad stand for five minutes to allow the bread to soften slightly.
5. Line a serving dish with the lettuce and transfer the salad into it. Garnish with basil and serve immediately.

CHICKEN AND SPINACH PIZZAS

Feed them spinach the smart way. Pizzas are forgiven every time!

Ingredients

2 (eight-inch) pizza breads
300 grams minced chicken (*keema*)
1 medium bunch (250 grams) fresh spinach (*palak*), chopped
2 tablespoons olive oil
1 large onion, chopped
4-5 garlic cloves, chopped
¼ teaspoon dried mixed herbs
1 teaspoon red chilli flakes
2 large tomatoes, blanched and chopped
Salt to taste
¼ cup tomato purée

Topping

2 cups grated mozzarella cheese
2 teaspoons red chilli flakes
1 teaspoon dried oregano
4 teaspoons olive oil

Method

1. Preheat the oven to 220°C/425°F/Gas Mark 7.
2. For the sauce, heat the olive oil in a pan; add the onion and garlic and sauté for a few minutes. Add the mixed herbs, chilli flakes and minced chicken and sauté over a moderate heat for two to three minutes.
3. Add the tomatoes and salt, and sauté for a minute. Cover the pan and cook over a low heat till the chicken is tender.
4. Add the spinach and continue to cook for another two minutes. Add the tomato purée, stir, adjust seasoning and simmer for two to three minutes till the mixture attains a thick, dropping consistency. Remove from heat and set aside.
5. Spread the pizza sauce on the pizza breads and top with the grated mozzarella cheese. Sprinkle chilli flakes and oregano and drizzle olive oil on top. Place on a greased baking tray and bake till the cheese melts and starts bubbling.
6. Remove from the oven, cut each pizza into four to six wedges and serve hot.

MINESTRONE TOSCANO WITH PESTO CRÔUTE

Busy cooks are grateful for chunky soups like this one, which is the perfect meal-in-a-bowl.

Ingredients

2 tablespoons macaroni
3 cups Vegetable Stock (page 98)
1 medium potato, cut into small pieces
1 medium carrot, cut into small pieces
3-4 French beans, cut into small pieces
Salt to taste
½ teaspoon white pepper powder
¼ small cabbage, shredded
1 medium zucchini, cut into small pieces
2 tablespoons Tomato Concasse (page 39)
½ cup tomato purée
1½ tablespoons olive oil
6-8 garlic cloves, chopped
1 medium onion, chopped
¼ teaspoon crushed dried oregano
10-12 fresh basil leaves (*tulsi ke patte*), roughly torn
½ cup grated Parmesan cheese

Method

1. Bring the vegetable stock to a boil in a deep pan. Add the macaroni and potato and cook over a moderate heat for a minute.
2. Add the carrot and French beans and continue to cook for a while. Add the salt and white pepper powder and mix. Add the cabbage, zucchini, tomato concasse and tomato purée.
3. Meanwhile, heat the olive oil in a pan. Add the garlic and onion and sauté till translucent. Add the oregano and continue to sauté. Add to the soup and stir to mix.
4. Add the basil and continue to simmer till the vegetables are cooked. Sprinkle Parmesan cheese and serve piping hot with pesto crôute.

Note:

To make pesto crôute, first toast bread slices and then apply Pesto (page 37). Or serve with Garlic Bread (page 76), or breadsticks.

SWEETCORN SOUP WITH MIXED VEGETABLES AND TOFU

Chunky nourishing soup... the perfect meal in a bowl.

Ingredients

150 grams cream-style sweetcorn
½ cup sweetcorn kernels (*makai ke dane*)
¼ small cabbage, chopped
¼ medium carrot, chopped
100 grams tofu (bean curd), cut into ½-inch pieces
2 tablespoons oil
4-5 cups Vegetable Stock (page 98)
Salt to taste
¼ teaspoon white pepper powder
½ tablespoon sugar
¼ teaspoon MSG (optional)
3 tablespoons cornflour
1 stalk spring onion greens, chopped

Method

1. Heat the oil in a wok; add the corn kernels, cabbage and carrot and stir-fry for two minutes. Stir in the vegetable stock and bring to a boil.
2. Mix in the cream-style corn and continue to cook for two to three minutes.
3. Add the salt, white pepper powder, sugar and MSG. Add the tofu and stir in the cornflour, mixed with half a cup of water. Cook over a high heat, stirring continuously, for one minute, or until the soup thickens.
4. Serve piping hot, garnished with spring onion greens.

PAV BHAJI ROLL-UPS

My favourite food...try it with tortillas for a quick bite.

Ingredients

4 tortillas
8 lettuce leaves

Pav bhaji

3 tablespoons oil
2 medium onions, chopped
3-4 green chillies, chopped
2 teaspoons ginger paste
2 teaspoons garlic paste
4 medium tomatoes, chopped
1 medium green capsicum (*hari Shimla mirch*), chopped
¼ cup shelled green peas, boiled and mashed lightly
¼ small cauliflower, grated
4 medium potatoes, boiled and grated
1½ tablespoons *pav bhaji masala*
Salt to taste
2 tablespoons chopped fresh coriander (*hara dhania*)

Onion-cheese mixture

1 large onion, sliced
2 large tomatoes, seeded and sliced
1 cup grated processed cheese
½ teaspoon red chilli powder

Method

1. To make the *pav bhaji*, heat the oil in a pan and add three-fourths of the onions. Sauté till light brown. Add the green chillies, ginger paste and garlic paste and sauté for half a minute. Add half the tomatoes and cook over a moderate heat, stirring continuously, for three to four minutes, or till the oil separates from the *masala*.
2. Add the capsicum, peas, cauliflower, potatoes and one and a half cups of water. Bring to a boil and simmer for ten minutes, pressing with the back of the ladle a few times, till all the vegetables are completely mashed.
3. Add the *pav bhaji masala*, salt and the remaining tomatoes. Cook over a moderate heat for two minutes, stirring continuously. Transfer the *bhaji* to a *kadai* and simmer for five to ten minutes, stirring often, till all the moisture evaporates and the *bhaji* is quite dry. Add the chopped coriander and mix. Transfer to a bowl and set aside.
4. Mix all the ingredients for the onion-cheese mixture together.
5. Heat a *tawa* and lightly warm the tortillas on both sides. Place a warmed tortilla on a square piece of aluminium foil. Spread one-fourth of the *bhaji* over the tortilla and generously sprinkle one-fourth of the onion-cheese mixture over it. Place two lettuce leaves at one end of the tortilla and roll up tightly. Wrap in the foil and serve.

PENNE IN THOUSAND ISLAND DRESSING

Simple meals are always welcome. Ready in a jiffy, eaten up even faster!

Ingredients

1 cup penne (quill-shaped pasta), boiled
½ cup Thousand Island Dressing (page 98)
1 medium carrot, cut into large pieces
¼ small broccoli, separated into small florets
3-4 French beans, cut diagonally into large pieces
1 tablespoon olive oil
½ medium green capsicum (*hari Shimla mirch*), cut into small triangles
1 medium onion, quartered
10-12 cherry tomatoes, halved
4-5 stuffed olives

Method

1. Blanch the carrot, broccoli and French beans separately. Refresh in cold water and drain.
2. Toss the pasta in the olive oil in a large mixing bowl.
3. Add the capsicum, onion, blanched vegetables, cherry tomatoes and stuffed olives.
4. Pour in the Thousand Island dressing, toss lightly and serve chilled.

CHEESY MACARONI

Make a large dish, because adults turn into kids when they get their hands on this!

Ingredients

1 cup grated processed cheese
300 grams macaroni, boiled
6 tablespoons butter
2 tablespoons refined flour (*maida*)
2 cups milk
Salt to taste
White pepper powder to taste
2 tablespoons fresh breadcrumbs
½ teaspoon crushed black peppercorns (*kali mirch*)
½ tablespoon chopped fresh parsley (*ajmoda*)

Method

1. Preheat the oven to 220°C/425°F/Gas Mark 7.
2. Heat two tablespoons of butter in a pan; add the flour and sauté lightly, making sure that it does not change colour.
3. Gradually add the milk, stirring continuously, so that no lumps form.
4. Add half the grated cheese and continue to stir. After adding the cheese, the sauce will thicken further, so add more milk to adjust the consistency.
5. Add salt and white pepper powder and mix well.
6. Heat two tablespoons of butter in a separate pan. Add the macaroni and toss to mix. Strain the sauce into the pan and mix gently.
7. Add the remaining cheese and transfer the mixture into a seven-inch square baking dish. Sprinkle breadcrumbs over the top and dot with the remaining butter. Sprinkle the crushed peppercorns and parsley. Bake till the cheese melts and turns golden brown. Serve hot.

CHICKEN AND SPINACH BAKE

Baked to perfection, this combination of chicken with greens is delicious. Serve with warm bread.

Ingredients

4 (200 grams each) boneless chicken breasts
2 bunches (500 grams) spinach (*palak*), blanched and chopped
Salt to taste
1 teaspoon black pepper (*kali mirch*) powder
½ teaspoon dried oregano
1 teaspoon vinegar (*sirka*)
¼ teaspoon mustard paste
¼ teaspoon sugar
2 tablespoons oil
¼ cup raw rice, soaked
½ cup milk
½ cup grated processed cheese
1 small onion, chopped
¼ cup breadcrumbs
2 tablespoons butter

Method

1. Preheat the oven to 200°C/400°F/Gas Mark 6.
2. Mix together the salt, pepper powder, oregano, vinegar, mustard paste and sugar. Rub the mixture all over the chicken and marinate for an hour preferably in a refrigerator.
3. Heat the oil in a pan and sauté the chicken breasts until both sides are golden brown.
4. Mix together the spinach, rice, milk, half the cheese, onion and salt in a large bowl. Spread the mixture at the bottom of a seven-inch square baking dish. Place the chicken on top of the spinach mixture.
5. Combine the breadcrumbs, butter and remaining cheese in a small bowl and sprinkle the mixture evenly over the chicken. Cover the dish with aluminium foil and bake for fifteen minutes.
6. Remove the foil and continue baking for five minutes, or until the spinach mixture has set and the chicken is no longer pink in the centre. Serve hot.

SPAGHETTI WITH CHICKEN AND PESTO

Pretty, rich and filling. That's pesto-flavoured chicken, especially if served with tangy mango salsa.

Ingredients

2 (200 grams each) chicken breasts, cut into 1-inch pieces
200 grams spaghetti, boiled and drained
2 tablespoons olive oil
Salt to taste

Pesto

1 cup fresh basil (*tulsi ke patte*)
5-6 garlic cloves
¼ cup pine nuts (*chilgoze*)
Salt to taste
2 tablespoons olive oil
⅓ cup Parmesan cheese shavings
3 tablespoons White Sauce (page 99)
¼ cup milk

Method

1. To make the pesto sauce, process the basil, garlic, pine nuts, salt and two tablespoons of olive oil in a blender till smooth. Add the Parmesan cheese and process again.
2. Thin the white sauce with the milk and transfer to a pan and set aside.
3. Heat half a tablespoon of olive oil in a pan; add the spaghetti and toss to coat with the oil. Sprinkle a little salt and toss till heated through. Spread the spaghetti on a serving plate.
4. Heat the remaining olive oil; add the chicken and sauté for two to three minutes. Add the pesto and sauté over a high heat. Add the white sauce and mix well. Season with salt and mix again. Cook for a few minutes till the chicken is tender.
5. Pour the sauce along with the chicken over the spaghetti and serve immediately.

BAKED MIXED VEGETABLES

Assemble before hand, give it twenty minutes to bake to an appetising golden colour and dig in!

Ingredients

3 medium brinjals (*baingan*), sliced
4 medium potatoes, boiled and sliced
1 medium green capsicum (*hari Shimla mirch*), sliced
1 medium red capsicum (*lal Shimla mirch*), sliced
Salt to taste
2 tablespoons oil
2 medium onions, cut into round slices, rings separated
¼ cup Vegetable Stock (page 98)
10-12 black peppercorns (*kali mirch*), crushed
½ cup fresh breadcrumbs
½ cup grated processed cheese

Tomato sauce

1 cup tomato concasse (see below)
2 tablespoons oil
3-4 garlic cloves, chopped
4-5 black peppercorns (*kali mirch*)
1 bay leaf (*tej patta*)
Salt to taste

Cheese sauce

½ cup White Sauce (page 99)
¼ cup grated processed cheese

Method

1. Preheat the oven to 200°C/400°F/Gas Mark 6.
2. Sprinkle salt on the brinjal slices. Place in a colander for thirty minutes to drain. Rinse under cold running water and pat dry with paper towels.
3. Arrange the brinjal slices on a baking tray and grill in the preheated oven till golden brown.
4. Heat two tablespoons of oil in a pan. Add the onion rings and sauté for a minute. Add the green and red capsicums and sauté for one or two minutes. Set aside.
5. For the tomato sauce, heat the oil in a pan. Add the garlic and sauté for one minute. Add the tomato concasse and sauté for two or three minutes. Add the peppercorns, bay leaf and salt and continue to cook for two or three minutes, or till the sauce thickens.
6. To make the cheese sauce, add the grated cheese to the white sauce and mix well.
7. Add the cheese sauce to the tomato sauce; add one-fourth cup of vegetable stock and bring the mixture to a boil. Remove from heat and strain.
8. In a seven-inch square baking dish, layer the onions, green and red capsicums followed by the brinjals and potatoes. Sprinkle salt and crushed peppercorns over each layer. Pour the tomato-cheese sauce over all the vegetables.
9. Sprinkle the fresh breadcrumbs and top with the grated cheese. Bake for about twenty minutes, or till the cheese turns golden brown.
10. Serve hot with brown bread.

Note:

To make 1 cup of tomato concasse, blanch 5 medium tomatoes in plenty of boiling water for two minutes. Drain and refresh in cold water; peel, cut in half, remove the seeds and chop roughly.

CHILLI-LEMON STEWED VEGETABLES WITH NOODLES

Chilli and lemon add a spicy tang to everyone's favourite noodles.

Ingredients

2 green chillies, sliced
2 lemon grass stalks, chopped
1 tablespoon lemon juice
7-8 cauliflower florets, finely sliced
7-8 fresh button mushrooms, finely sliced
¼ cup sweetcorn kernels (*makai ke dane*)
1 small green capsicum (*hari Shimla mirch*), cut into ½-inch pieces
½ medium red capsicum (*lal Shimla mirch*), cut into ½-inch pieces
½ medium yellow capsicum (*pili Shimla mirch*), cut into ½-inch pieces
¼ cup bean sprouts
2 medium tomatoes, cut into 1-inch pieces
¼ cup boiled noodles
3 tablespoons oil
4 cups Vegetable Stock (page 98)
1 teaspoon cornflour
Salt to taste
5-6 black peppercorns (*kali mirch*), crushed

Method

1. Heat one tablespoon of oil in a wok. Add the noodles and sauté till light brown. Transfer to a serving dish and keep warm.
2. Heat the remaining oil in the wok. Add the green chillies and lemon grass and sauté for a minute. Add the cauliflower, mushrooms, corn, capsicums, bean sprouts and tomatoes and stir-fry for a few minutes.
3. Stir in the vegetable stock and bring the mixture to a boil. Add the cornflour mixed in one tablespoon of water and stir. Cook till the mixture thickens slightly.
4. Add the salt, crushed peppercorns and lemon juice and mix gently. Pour over the noodles and serve hot.

DAL DHOKLI

Comfort food, thy name is dhokli. I suggest you add some chopped fresh spinach to the dhokli dough.

Ingredients

¾ cup split pigeon peas (*arhar dal/toovar dal*)
¾ cup wholewheat flour (*atta*)
2 tablespoons gram flour (*besan*)
Salt to taste
¾ teaspoon turmeric powder (*haldi*)
¾ teaspoon red chilli powder
2 pinches asafoetida (*hing*)
½ tablespoon oil
1½ tablespoons raw peanuts (*moongphali*)
1 tablespoon pure *ghee*
¼ teaspoon mustard seeds (*rai*)
½ teaspoon cumin seeds (*jeera*)
4 garlic cloves, chopped
4-5 curry leaves
3 *kokum* rinds
1½ teaspoons grated jaggery (*gur*)
2 tablespoons chopped fresh coriander (*hara dhania*)

Method

1. Soak the *toovar dal* in two cups of water for half an hour.
2. Mix the wholewheat flour and gram flour. Add the salt, one-fourth teaspoon turmeric powder, chilli powder, a pinch of asafoetida, oil and sufficient water to knead into a hard dough. Roll out thin *rotis* of the dough and cut into diamonds (*dhokli*).
3. Boil the *dal* with one and a half cups of water. When half cooked, add the peanuts and remaining turmeric powder. Set aside.
4. Heat the *ghee* in a pan; add the mustard seeds, cumin seeds, remaining asafoetida, garlic and curry leaves. Pour the sizzling spices into the *dal*.
5. Add two cups of water and the *kokum* and bring to a boil. Add the jaggery and cook, stirring till the jaggery dissolves. Add the *dhokli* and cook, stirring occasionally, so that they do not stick to the bottom of the pan. Simmer till the *dhokli* are cooked.
6. Serve hot, garnished with the chopped coriander.

FRITTATA WITH CARAMELISED ONIONS AND ROASTED PEPPERS

Eggs are handy when there are emergencies or when the cook is struck by a bout of laziness. Ensure there is lots of ketchup to go around!

Ingredients

4 large eggs
2 large onions, sliced
1 medium red capsicum (*lal Shimla mirch*)
1 medium yellow capsicum (*pili Shimla mirch*)
Salt to taste
1 medium potato
2 tablespoons butter
¼ teaspoon sugar
20-25 spinach leaves (*palak*), chopped
8 black peppercorns (*kali mirch*), crushed

Method

1. Preheat the grill.
2. To roast the capsicums, cut in half lengthways and remove the seeds. Place the halves, cut side down, on a baking sheet and grill until the skins blacken and blister. Remove, cover loosely with aluminium foil and leave to stand for ten minutes. Peel the skins and slice the capsicums.
3. Bring three cups of water to a boil in a deep pan. Add the salt and potato, cover and cook till tender. Drain and set aside to cool. Peel, halve lengthways and slice the potato.
4. Melt the butter in a thick-bottomed frying pan. Add the onions, sugar and a pinch of salt. Sauté until the onions brown and caramelise. Add the spinach and continue to sauté for one or two minutes.
5. Whisk together the eggs, salt and crushed peppercorns in a bowl.
6. Arrange the potato slices overlapping each other, at the bottom of a non-stick frying pan.
7. Scatter half the caramelised onions and half the roasted capsicums over the potatoes.
8. Pour the eggs over, even the surface and top with the remaining onions and capsicums. Set aside for fifteen to twenty minutes so that the potatoes absorb some of the egg.
9. Place the frying pan over a moderate heat. Cook, shaking the pan often, until the bottom of the frittata is lightly browned. Slide the frittata onto a large plate, turn it over and slide it back into the pan to cook the other side. Cook for another two minutes.
10. Transfer to a large plate and cut into wedges when slightly cooled. Serve immediately.

HARIYALI TIKKI WITH CHOLE

Make this dish in advance. Just before serving, heat up the chole and you are done!

Ingredients

Tikkis

2 bunches (500 grams) fresh spinach (*palak*), blanched and chopped
4 medium potatoes, boiled and mashed
½ teaspoon red chilli powder
½ teaspoon roasted cumin (*bhuna jeera*) powder
2 tablespoons cornflour
Salt to taste
Oil for shallow-frying

Chole

1 cup chickpeas (*kabuli chana*), soaked and boiled
1 large onion, chopped
3-4 green chillies
1 tablespoon coriander (*dhania*) powder
1 teaspoon red chilli powder
½ teaspoon turmeric (*haldi*) powder
1 teaspoon *garam masala* powder
2 tablespoons oil
1 medium tomato, chopped
Salt to taste

To serve

1 medium onion, chopped
1 medium tomato, chopped
1 tablespoon chopped fresh coriander (*hara dhania*)

Method

1. For the *tikki*, mix together the spinach, potatoes, chilli powder, cumin powder, cornflour and salt. Divide into eight portions and shape into *tikki*.
2. Heat the oil in a frying pan and shallow-fry the *tikki* till evenly browned on both sides. Drain on absorbent paper.
3. For the *chole*, grind together the onion, green chillies, coriander powder, chilli powder, turmeric powder and *garam masala* powder.
4. Heat the oil in a *kadai*. Add the ground paste and sauté for five to eight minutes till well browned.
5. Add the tomato and salt, stir well and cook till the oil separates. Add the *kabuli chana* and cook for about five minutes. Add one cup of liquid in which the *chole* was cooked. Stir well and boil for two minutes. Remove from heat.
6. To serve, arrange the *tikki* on a plate. Top with the *chole*, sprinkle chopped onion, tomato and coriander. Serve hot.

WHOLESOME SPAGHETTI

Peppers, spinach, chicken and cheese meet with wholewheat pasta...read on for the happy ending!

Ingredients

100 grams wholewheat spaghetti
Salt to taste
2 tablespoons oil
250 grams boneless chicken breasts, cut into 1-inch pieces
1 teaspoon Worcestershire sauce
4½ tablespoons olive oil
6-8 garlic cloves, chopped
¼ cup tomato ketchup
1 small green capsicum (*hari Shimla mirch*), cut into 1-inch pieces
1 small red capsicum (*lal Shimla mirch*), cut into 1-inch pieces
1 small yellow capsicum (*pili Shimla mirch*), cut into 1-inch pieces
1 teaspoon black pepper (*kali mirch*) powder
5-6 fresh basil leaves (*tulsi ke patte*), roughly torn
1 large onion, chopped
4-5 fresh button mushrooms, sliced
½ cup blanched and chopped spinach (*palak*)
3 tablespoons cream
1 cup White Sauce (page 99)
1 cup grated mozzarella cheese

Method

1. Boil spaghetti in plenty of salted water till *al dente* (cooked, but firm to the bite). Drain, add the oil and toss to coat with the oil.
2. Marinate the chicken pieces in the Worcestershire sauce.
3. Heat equal quantities of olive oil in two separate pans. Add an equal quantity of garlic to both the pans and sauté for a few minutes.
4. Add the marinated chicken to one pan and sauté for five minutes. Add the tomato ketchup and mix. Add the capsicums, salt, half the pepper powder and the basil. Cook till the chicken is tender and remove from heat.
5. Add the onion to the other pan and sauté for a while. Add the mushrooms and continue to sauté for two to three minutes. Add the spinach, cream, salt and remaining pepper powder and mix. Remove from heat.
6. Preheat the oven to 200°C/400°F/Gas Mark 6.
7. Spread half the white sauce at the bottom of a baking dish. Spread half the spaghetti over it and cover with the spinach and mushroom mixture.
8. Sprinkle half the mozzarella cheese and cover with the remaining spaghetti and the white sauce. Spread the chicken mixture and cover with the remaining mozzarella cheese.
9. Bake for fifteen minutes till the cheese is bubbly and golden brown. Serve hot.

TACOS WITH REFRIED BEANS, SALSA AND CRISPY VEGETABLES

A cowboy film? Bring on the tacos please!

Ingredients

8 taco shells
2 cups soaked red kidney beans (*rajma*)
4 garlic cloves
1 bay leaf (*tej patta*)
3 tablespoons oil
3 medium onions, chopped
Salt to taste
10-12 black peppercorns (*kali mirch*), freshly ground
½ small head iceberg lettuce, shredded
1 medium carrot, grated
½ small red cabbage, shredded
¼ cup Salsa (page 53)
½ cup grated Cheddar cheese

Method

1. Place the kidney beans in a large pan with the garlic and bay leaf. Cover with cold water and bring to a boil. Lower the heat and cook gently until the beans are very tender.
2. Drain the beans, reserving the cooking liquid. Discard the bay leaf.
3. Mash the beans coarsely with a potato masher or process in a blender or food processor, adding some of the reserved liquid.
4. Heat the oil in a pan; add the onions and sauté till translucent. Add the beans, salt and pepper and mix well. Simmer for a few minutes. Take the pan off the heat and keep warm.
5. Mix together the iceberg lettuce, carrot and red cabbage. Place in a refrigerator to chill.
6. Spoon the refried beans into each taco shell. Top with the salsa and sprinkle with cheese. Top with the chilled vegetables and serve immediately.

TEX-MEX PASTA

Fuse some Italian with Mexican and come up with a blockbuster!

Ingredients

200 grams fettuccine (narrow, flat pasta ribbons)
1 tablespoon oil
2 tablespoons garlic and chilli-flavoured olive oil
½ medium zucchini, cut into strips
1 small red capsicum (*lal Shimla mirch*), cut into strips
1 small yellow capsicum (*pili Shimla mirch*), cut into strips
1 small green capsicum (*hari Shimla mirch*), cut into strips
Salt to taste

Salsa

1½ tablespoons oil
4 cloves garlic, crushed
1 small onion, chopped
2 fresh red chillies, chopped
½ small green capsicum (*hari Shimla mirch*), chopped
½ teaspoon roasted cumin (*bhuna jeera*) powder
1 teaspoon red chilli powder
1 cup tomato purée
Salt to taste
1 tablespoon lemon juice
2 tablespoons chopped fresh coriander (*hara dhania*)

To serve

8-10 tortilla chips
1 cup mozzarella cheese, grated
2 jalapeño chillies, sliced

Method

1. Preheat the oven to 180°C/350°F/Gas Mark 4.
2. Bring plenty of water to boil and cook the pasta in it for five to seven minutes or till *al dente* (cooked, but firm to the bite), stirring gently. Drain, refresh in cold water and drain again. Add the oil and toss to coat the pasta.
3. For the salsa, heat the oil and sauté the garlic and onion. Add the red chillies, capsicum, roasted cumin powder, chilli powder and tomato purée. Stir well and add salt to taste. Cook for two to three minutes and remove from heat. When cool, stir in the lemon juice and chopped coriander.
4. In a separate pan, heat the garlic and chilli-flavoured olive oil; add the zucchini and capsicum strips. Add salt to taste and stir-fry for three to four minutes. Add the boiled fettuccine and mix well. Add the salsa and mix well.
5. Crumble the tortilla chips and arrange in a layer at the bottom of a seven-inch square baking dish. Spread the pasta over the chips and cover with the grated mozzarella cheese. Scatter the jalapeño chillies on top and bake for six to seven minutes, or till the cheese melts completely. Serve hot.

STIR-FRIED MEDLEY

Stir-fries and sitcoms go hand in hand...

Ingredients

150 grams extra firm tofu (bean curd), cut into ½-inch cubes
4-5 broccoli florets
1 tablespoon sliced celery
1 medium green capsicum (*hari Shimla mirch*), sliced
½ medium red capsicum (*lal Shimla mirch*), sliced
1 leek, sliced
3-4 fresh button mushrooms, sliced
2 garlic cloves
¼ inch ginger
1½ tablespoons oil
2 tablespoons roasted peanuts (*bhuni moongphali*), crushed
1 tablespoon soy sauce
1 tablespoon tomato sauce
A dash of red chilli sauce
1½ teaspoons lemon juice
1½ teaspoons cornflour
½ cup fresh pineapple (*ananas*) chunks

Method

1. Pound the garlic and ginger to a paste.
2. Heat the oil in a pan and sauté the ginger-garlic paste and tofu till lightly browned. Drain and set aside.
3. To the same pan, add the broccoli, celery, capsicums, leek, mushrooms and peanuts. Stir-fry till the vegetables are tender, but remain crisp.
4. Mix together the soy sauce, tomato sauce, chilli sauce, lemon juice and cornflour. Add to the pan and cook, stirring continuously, till well mixed.
5. Add the tofu and pineapple and mix gently. Serve hot with boiled rice.

QUICK JEERA CHICKEN

Short work in the kitchen but excellent results! Have this ideally with roti. Pav or brown bread will also do.

Ingredients

1 teaspoon cumin seeds (*jeera*)
1 whole (800 grams) chicken, cut into 1½-inch pieces
2 tablespoons oil
4-5 green chillies, sliced
2 medium onions, sliced
1 teaspoon red chilli powder
½ teaspoon turmeric (*haldi*) powder
Salt to taste
1 tablespoon lemon juice
2 tablespoons chopped fresh coriander (*hara dhania*)
1 tablespoon roughly torn fresh mint (*pudina*)

Method

1. Heat the oil in a *kadai*. Add the cumin seeds and sauté till they begin to change colour. Add the green chillies and onions and sauté till golden brown.
2. Add the chicken and stir. Cover the pan and cook over a moderate heat for ten minutes.
3. Add the chilli powder, turmeric powder and salt and mix well. Cover again and cook for another ten minutes, or till the chicken is tender.
4. Stir in the lemon juice, coriander and mint. Serve hot with *roti*.

SHANGHAI STEWED NOODLES

Soft noodles with a saucy coating...perfect with that mushy serial.

Ingredients

200 grams noodles
1 tablespoon oil
6-8 garlic cloves, crushed
1 medium onion, sliced
1 spring onion, sliced
½ medium carrot, halved and sliced
4 fresh button mushrooms, sliced
¼ small cabbage, cut into 1-inch pieces
½ medium green capsicum (*hari Shimla mirch*), cut into 1-inch pieces
5 cups Vegetable Stock (page 98)
1½ tablespoons cornflour
¼ teaspoon MSG (optional)
½ teaspoon white pepper powder
Salt to taste
1 stalk spring onion greens, sliced
2 tablespoons chilli oil

Method

1. Heat the oil in a wok; add the garlic, onion and spring onion and stir-fry for a few minutes. Add the carrot, mushrooms, cabbage and capsicum and continue to stir-fry for a minute.
2. Add the vegetable stock, bring to a boil and add the noodles. Cook over a high heat for two minutes. Lower the heat and simmer for four to five minutes, or until the noodles are almost cooked.
3. Mix the cornflour with half a cup of water. Stir the MSG, white pepper powder, salt to taste and cornflour mixture into the noodles. Cook, stirring frequently, over a moderate heat for a couple of minutes or until the sauce thickens.
4. Add the spring onion greens, drizzle the chilli oil and serve hot.

SOYA GRANULE LASAGNE

Pasta layered with a protein-rich filling and a cheesy herb sauce... a marvellous combination for those who do not like spicy food.

Ingredients

1 cup soya granules, soaked
8 (140 grams) lasagne sheets
Salt to taste
3 tablespoons olive oil
3 tablespoons milk
3-4 garlic cloves, chopped
1 medium onion, chopped
3 medium tomatoes, chopped
½ cup tomato ketchup
1 cup White Sauce (page 99)
4-5 fresh basil leaves (*tulsi ke patte*)
2 teaspoons crushed red chillies
½ cup grated processed cheese
¼ teaspoon mixed herbs

Method

1. Boil seven to eight cups of water in a large wide-mouthed pan. Add a little salt. Slide in the lasagne sheets and cook till *al dente* (cooked, but still firm to the bite). Drain and refresh in cold water.
2. Heat two tablespoons of olive oil in a separate pan. Add the soaked soya granules and the milk and cook for three or four minutes. Add salt, mix and set aside.
3. To make the sauce, heat the remaining oil in a separate pan. Add the garlic and sauté for a minute. Add the onion and sauté till translucent. Add the tomatoes and cook till pulpy. Add the tomato ketchup and cook for one minute longer. Stir in the white sauce and bring to a boil. Adjust salt. Remove from heat and add the basil and half the crushed red chillies and mix well.
4. Preheat the oven to 180°C/350°F/Gas Mark 4.
5. Spread some of the sauce at the bottom of a seven-inch square baking dish. Cut the lasagne sheets to the size of the baking dish. Cover the sauce with two lasagne sheets. Spread half the soya mixture over it. Place two lasagne sheets over the soya layer.
6. Repeat the layers once more taking care to end with the sauce layer. Spread the grated cheese evenly over the sauce.
7. Sprinkle with the remaining crushed red chillies and mixed herbs. Bake for at least twenty-five minutes or till the cheese layer is golden brown. Serve hot.

SPINACH AND CHEESE PIE

Palak and paneer in a crusty cocoon...fusion food at its best!

Ingredients

500 grams fresh spinach (*palak*), stems removed
225 grams cottage cheese (*paneer*), grated
1 cup refined flour (*maida*)
60 grams chilled butter, chopped
1 tablespoon olive oil
2 small onions, chopped
1 tablespoon chopped fresh oregano or ½ teaspoon dried oregano
Freshly ground black pepper (*kali mirch*) powder to taste
Salt to taste
A pinch of grated nutmeg (*jaiphal*)
½ cup cream
½ cup milk
1 egg

Method

1. Preheat the oven to 180°C/350°F/Gas Mark 4.
2. Place the flour and chilled butter in a food processor and process until the mixture resembles coarse breadcrumbs. If mixing by hand, rub the butter into the flour with your fingertips.
3. With the processor motor running, add drops of iced water until the dough comes together. If not using a processor, mix with a knife or a wooden spoon. Or mix lightly with your hands. You will need approximately two and a half tablespoons of water.
4. Press the dough into a ball, wrap in greaseproof paper or cling wrap and refrigerate for at least thirty minutes before rolling or shaping.
5. Cut the spinach into thin ribbons with a sharp knife.
6. Heat the oil in a large pan. Add the onions and sauté over a moderate heat for five minutes, or until softened. Add the spinach, oregano, pepper powder, salt and nutmeg and cook over a high heat, stirring frequently for about five minutes, or until most of the liquid has evaporated. Remove from heat and set aside to cool.
7. To make the custard, whisk together the cream, milk, egg and a pinch of salt. Set aside.
8. Roll out the dough into a half-inch thick disc. Line a pie dish with the rolled out pastry and trim the edges. Prick with a fork and bake blind for twenty-five minutes.
9. Spread the spinach mixture over the pastry and top with the cottage cheese. Pour the custard mixture over and bake for thirty-five to forty minutes.
10. Cut into wedges and serve hot.

MISSAL PAV

Missal! Hot and spicy just like the movie on TV!

Ingredients

8 *pav*
1 cup sprouted green gram (*ankurit moong*)
1 cup sprouted brown gram (*ankurit moth*)
2 tablespoons oil
A pinch of asafoetida (*hing*)
½ teaspoon mustard seeds (*rai*)
A few curry leaves (*kadi patta*)
2 large onions, finely chopped
2 green chillies, slit
1 teaspoon garlic paste
1 teaspoon ginger paste
½ teaspoon turmeric (*haldi*) powder
1½ teaspoons red chilli powder
1 teaspoon coriander-cumin (*dhania-jeera*) powder
Salt to taste
1 teaspoon *garam masala* powder
2 tablespoons fresh coriander (*hara dhania*), finely chopped
½ cup *farsan*
Lemon juice, as required
Lemon wedges, as required

Method

1. Mix the sprouted gram in a colander and wash under running water for one minute. Drain.
2. Heat the oil in a pan; add the asafoetida, mustard seeds, curry leaves and half the onions. Sauté for one minute and add the green chillies, garlic paste and ginger paste. Stir well and sprinkle a little water.
3. Add the turmeric powder, chilli powder and coriander-cumin powder. Mix well and add the sprouted gram. Add salt to taste and three cups of water and bring to a boil.
4. Add the *garam masala* powder and chopped coriander, reserving some for garnishing. Cover and cook for ten to twelve minutes.
5. To serve, place a ladleful of cooked sprouted gram in each small, deep bowl. Sprinkle generously with *farsan*. Sprinkle the remaining onion, remaining coriander and the lemon juice over the *farsan*.
6. Serve with lemon wedges and *pav*.

MULTI-GRAIN FOOT-LONG WITH MUSHROOMS AND CHICKEN SALAMI

Take the makings of the sandwich to the table and assemble while watching your favourite programme on the tube.

Ingredients

1 multi-grain long loaf
10-12 medium fresh button mushrooms, sliced
6 slices chicken salami
1 tablespoon oil
Salt to taste
8-10 black peppercorns (*kali mirch*), crushed
2 tablespoons Mayonnaise (page 99)
8 lettuce leaves, shredded
¼ cup sliced black olives
1 small onion, sliced
5-6 pickled gherkins, sliced
2 cheese slices
Tomato ketchup, as required
Mustard sauce, as required

Method

1. Heat the oil in a pan. Add the mushrooms and sauté over a high heat for one minute. Add salt and the crushed peppercorns. Sauté for one minute longer and remove from heat.
2. Slit the bread lengthways without cutting through.
3. Spread the insides with mayonnaise. Cover the bottom half with shredded lettuce.
4. Arrange the sliced black olives, onion and pickled gherkins on the lettuce. Cut the cheese slices into two and place on the toppings. Place the mushrooms and chicken salami on top.
5. Drizzle tomato ketchup and mustard sauce over the filling. Press the top half of the loaf down gently to enclose the filling. Cut into smaller pieces and serve immediately.

OODLES OF NOODLES

Another great meal-in-a-bowl. I love the crunch of corn in this dish.

Ingredients

200 grams noodles
1 tablespoon oil
2 spring onions, sliced
1 small yellow capsicum (*pili Shimla mirch*), sliced
1 small red capsicum (*lal Shimla mirch*), sliced
4-5 French beans, sliced diagonally and blanched
½ cup sweetcorn kernels (*makai ke dane*), boiled
2 teaspoons soy sauce
Salt to taste
2 tablespoons hot and sweet tomato ketchup
1 tablespoon sweet chilli sauce
¼ cup bean sprouts
2 stalks spring onion greens, sliced

Method

1. Boil the noodles in plenty of salted water. Drain, refresh in cold water and set aside.
2. Heat the oil in a pan; add the spring onions and stir-fry for a while. Add the capsicums and French beans and stir-fry for a few minutes.
3. Add the sweet corn and soy sauce and mix well. Add the noodles and salt and toss to mix.
4. Add the hot and sweet tomato ketchup and sweet chilli sauce and mix gently.
5. Add the bean sprouts and spring onion greens and mix well. Serve hot.

PAELLA WITH TOFU

Add a new, healthier note to the traditional Spanish dish.

Ingredients

1½ cups paella rice (or any short-grained rice), soaked
150 grams tofu (bean curd), cut into ½-inch cubes
3 tablespoons olive oil
1 medium onion, sliced
2 medium tomatoes, cut into ½-inch pieces
2 teaspoons red chilli powder
¼ teaspoon turmeric (*haldi*) powder
A few saffron threads (*kesar*)
3½ cups Vegetable Stock (page 98)
Salt to taste
¼ cup shelled green peas, blanched
1 medium red capsicum (*lal Shimla mirch*), cut into ½-inch pieces
1 medium green capsicum (*hari Shimla mirch*), cut into ½-inch pieces
2 tablespoons chopped fresh coriander (*hara dhania*)
2 lemons, cut into wedges

Method

1. Drain the soaked rice and set aside.
2. Heat two tablespoons of olive oil in a deep pan. Add the onion and sauté till translucent. Add the tomatoes and sauté for two minutes.
3. Add the chilli powder, turmeric powder and saffron and mix. Add the vegetable stock, salt and rice and mix again. Cook till the rice is half done.
4. Meanwhile, heat the remaining olive oil in a separate pan; add the green peas, capsicums and tofu and toss till lightly browned and crunchy.
5. Add to the rice and cook till the rice is tender. Serve hot, garnished with the chopped coriander and lemon wedges.

BROWN RICE BIRYANI WITH CHUTNEY CHICKEN

Pop it into the microwave and out comes an extremely satisfactory biryani!

Ingredients

2 cups brown Basmati rice, soaked
½ cup Green Chutney (page 98)
800 grams chicken on the bone, cut into 1½-inch pieces
Salt to taste
2 inches cinnamon (*dalchini*)
6 green cardamoms (*chhoti elaichi*)
8 cloves (*laung*)
½ cup yogurt (*dahi*)
¼ teaspoon turmeric powder (*haldi*)
5-6 saffron threads (*kesar*)
2 tablespoons milk
3 tablespoons oil
2 medium onions, sliced
1 teaspoon ginger paste
1 teaspoon garlic paste
3 tablespoons chopped fresh coriander (*hara dhania*)
A few rose petals
A few sprigs of fresh mint (*pudina*)
1 cup deep-fried onion slices
1 teaspoon *kewra* water
1 teaspoon rose water
½ teaspoon *garam masala* powder

Method

1. Cook the rice with salt, six cups of water, half the cinnamon, cardamoms and cloves till three-fourths done. Drain and set aside.
2. Place the green chutney in a bowl; add the yogurt, salt and turmeric powder and mix. Marinate the chicken in the mixture for an hour, preferably in a refrigerator. Soak the saffron in the milk.
3. Heat the oil in a deep pan; add the remaining cinnamon, cardamoms, cloves and sliced onions and sauté till the onions turn brown.
4. Add the ginger and garlic pastes and sauté, adding a little water to prevent scorching. Add the marinated chicken and mix well. Lower the heat, cover and cook for five minutes. Stir in the chopped coriander.
5. In a deep microwave-safe bowl, spread a layer of half the rice at the bottom. Sprinkle half the saffron-flavoured milk, rose petals, mint, fried onions, *kewra* water, rose water and *garam masala* powder over the rice. Spread the chicken with the gravy and again spread layers of the remaining rice, saffron-flavoured milk, rose petals, mint, fried onions, *kewra* water, rose water and *garam masala* powder.
6. Cover with cling wrap, pierced with a few holes to allow the steam to escape. Place in a microwave oven and cook on HIGH (100%) for five minutes.
7. Leave to stand in the oven for five minutes. Remove the cling wrap and serve hot with *raita*.

CHEESY RICE-STUFFED PEPPERS

Soft, succulent capsicums filled with cheesy rice. The perfect bite when a thriller's on the telly.

Ingredients

1 cup grated processed cheese
¾ cup rice, soaked
1 large red capsicum (*lal Shimla mirch*)
1 large yellow capsicum (*pili Shimla mirch*)
1 large green capsicum (*hari Shimla mirch*)
3 tablespoons olive oil
Salt to taste
1 medium onion, chopped
2-3 garlic cloves, chopped
2-inch leek stalk, chopped
¼ cup tomato purée
½ teaspoon red chilli powder
½ cup American corn kernels (*makai ke dane*)
1 jalapeño chilli, chopped

Method

1. Halve the capsicums lengthways leaving the stem intact. Remove the seeds and membranes, rub one tablespoon of oil and a little salt inside and outside the capsicum halves and set aside for about ten minutes.
2. Heat the remaining oil in a thick-bottomed pan; add the onions and sauté over a moderate heat for two minutes. Add the garlic and leek and continue to sauté for a minute.
3. Add the tomato purée, chilli powder and salt and cook over a low heat for one minute. Add the rice and two and a quarter cups of water and bring to a boil. Lower the heat, cover the pan and cook till almost done.
4. Stir in the corn and jalapeño chilli and cook for another three to four minutes, or till the water is absorbed. Add half a cup of grated cheese and stir gently with a fork.
5. Preheat the oven to 170°C/325°F/Gas Mark 3.
6. Fill each capsicum half with the rice mixture and sprinkle a little of the remaining cheese over each capsicum. Place on a greased baking tray and bake for fifteen minutes or till the capsicums have softened slightly. Serve hot.

CHICKEN STEW WITH GARLIC BREAD

Wholesome food, soul food, hot chicken stew! Kids will lap it up, vegetables and all.

Ingredients

1 kilogram boneless chicken, cut into 1½-inch cubes
3 tablespoons unsalted butter
8-10 garlic cloves, sliced
2 medium onions, sliced
2 medium carrots, cut into large pieces
2 medium potatoes, cut into large pieces
6-8 French beans, cut into 1-inch pieces
3 tablespoons wholewheat flour (*atta*)
Salt to taste
5 cups Chicken Stock (page 98)
½ teaspoon black pepper (*kali mirch*) powder
½ cup milk

Garlic bread

1 French loaf (*baguette*)
4 tablespoons salted butter
2 teaspoons garlic paste
5-6 black peppercorns (*kali mirch*), crushed

Method

1. Preheat the oven to 200°C/400°F/Gas Mark 6.
2. For the garlic bread, cream the butter till smooth; add the garlic paste and crushed peppercorns. Slit the French loaf diagonally two inches apart, and generously spread the butter between the slits. Wrap the loaf in aluminium foil and place in the hot oven for five to eight minutes.
3. For the chicken stew, heat the butter in a thick-bottomed pan. Add the garlic, onions, carrots and potatoes and sauté for four to five minutes over a high heat till all the moisture dries up.
4. Add the wholewheat flour and sauté for a minute. Add the chicken and salt and sauté for eight to ten minutes. Add the stock and bring the mixture to a boil. Stir in half the pepper powder, cover the pan and cook for three to four minutes.
5. Uncover the pan, add the French beans and cook till tender. Add the milk and the remaining pepper. Cover and cook over a moderate heat for seven to eight minutes.
6. Serve hot with the warm garlic bread.

CORN AND CORIANDER RICE

Running out of time? Here's a dish that can be made in a jiffy.

Ingredients

1 cup Basmati rice, soaked
¾ cup tinned corn kernels (*makai ke dane*)
6 tablespoons chopped fresh coriander (*hara dhania*)
2 tablespoons olive oil
2-3 garlic cloves, chopped
2 green chillies, seeded and chopped
Salt to taste
1 tablespoon lemon juice

Method

1. Cook the rice in three cups of water until just cooked. Drain thoroughly and spread on a large plate to cool.
2. Heat the olive oil in a wok; add the garlic and sauté for a minute.
3. Add the green chillies, rice, corn, chopped coriander, salt and lemon juice and sauté over a high heat for two to three minutes, stirring and tossing continuously.
4. Transfer to a serving bowl and serve hot with *raita*.

ERRA SAADAM

The exotic combination of prawns and fennel turns leftover rice into a feast.

Ingredients

2 cups steamed Basmati rice, cooled
2 eggs, beaten
450 grams small prawns (*jheenga*), peeled and deveined
2 tablespoons oil
½ teaspoon mustard seeds (*rai*)
1 clove (*laung*)
1 green cardamom (*chhoti elaichi*)
½ inch cinnamon (*dalchini*)
1 bay leaf (*tej patta*)
2 large onions, chopped
2 garlic cloves, chopped
2 medium tomatoes, cut into small pieces
½ teaspoon red chilli powder
Salt to taste
½ teaspoon turmeric powder (*haldi*)
4-5 black peppercorns (*kali mirch*), crushed
1 tablespoon fennel seeds (*saunf*), powdered
2 tablespoons chopped fresh coriander (*hara dhania*)

Method

1. Heat the oil in a non-stick pan. Add the mustard seeds, clove, cardamom, cinnamon and bay leaf and sauté till the mustard seeds begin to splutter. Add the onions and garlic and sauté for about five minutes, or until lightly browned.
2. Lower the heat and add the tomatoes. Cook, pressing the tomatoes with the back of a spoon, till all the moisture evaporates and the oil separates. Add the chilli powder, salt, turmeric powder and one-fourth of the crushed peppercorns and cook for a minute. Add the prawns and cook for five minutes, stirring occasionally.
3. Mix the powdered fennel, the remaining crushed peppercorns and a pinch of salt into the beaten eggs and pour over the prawns.
4. Cook for another minute, add the rice and cook for two to three minutes, or until the eggs are cooked and the prawns are pink.
5. Garnish with the chopped coriander and serve.

GOAN FISH CURRY WITH RED RICE

Fish curry with rice is like dal with roti: so comforting! If you think you are going to be too engrossed in the show on TV, make sure that you use boneless fish.

Ingredients

2 medium (400 grams each) pomfrets or any flat fish
2 tablespoons oil
1 small onion, chopped
2 green chillies, slit and halved
Salt to taste
1 tablespoon malt vinegar (*sirka*)

Masala

2 teaspoons cumin seeds (*jeera*)
2 tablespoons coriander seeds (*dhania*)
6 dried red chillies
½ cup grated coconut
2 inches ginger, chopped
15 garlic cloves, chopped
2 tablespoons tamarind (*imli*) pulp

Method

1. Clean, wash and slice each fish into five to six pieces across the bone.
2. For the *masala*, dry-roast the cumin seeds, coriander seeds and red chillies. Grind the roasted spices, grated coconut, ginger, garlic and tamarind with a little water to a paste.
3. Rub half the ground paste into the fish slices.
4. Heat the oil in a pan. Add the onions and sauté till golden brown. Add the green chillies and cook over a moderate heat for three minutes, stirring continuously.
5. Add the remaining ground *masala* and stir well. Sauté for five minutes till fragrant. Stir in one and a half cups of water and bring to a boil. Add the marinated fish and salt. Cook over a low heat for about five minutes or till the fish is tender.
6. Stir in the vinegar and serve hot with red rice.

Note:

Red rice, with its nutty flavour and plump grains, requires at least two hours of soaking before it is cooked. It is well worth the time as it is perfect with fish curry.

JAMMU KA ALOO-ANARDANA PARANTHA

Aloo paranthe with a dieter's touch! Brush liberally with butter for the kids...

Ingredients

2 large potatoes, boiled and mashed
1 teaspoon pomegranate seeds (*anardana*), roasted and powdered
2 cups wholewheat flour (*atta*)
Salt to taste
2 tablespoons milk
2 tablespoons yogurt (*dahi*)
1 small onion, chopped
½ teaspoon red chilli powder
2 green chillies, chopped
1 teaspoon *chaat masala*
2 tablespoons chopped fresh coriander (*hara dhania*)

Method

1. Place the wholewheat flour in a bowl; add the salt, milk, yogurt and sufficient water and knead into a soft dough. Cover with a damp cloth and set aside for fifteen minutes. Divide the dough into eight portions.
2. Add the onion to the mashed potatoes along with the chilli powder, green chillies, roasted *anardana* powder, *chaat masala*, chopped coriander and salt and mix well. Divide into eight portions.
3. Roll out each portion of the dough into a small *puri*; place one portion of potato stuffing in the centre, gather in the edges and roll into a ball. Roll out into a *parantha*.
4. Heat a *tawa*. Place a *parantha* on it and roast for half a minute. Flip over and moisten the top lightly with a little water. Flip over again and moisten the other side as well. Continue to cook till both sides are evenly browned.
5. Serve hot with fresh yogurt.

KESARI SEAFOOD PULAO

The twist is in the saffron, which reminds one of Spanish paella.

Ingredients

1½ cups Basmati rice
7-8 saffron threads (*kesar*)
7-8 mussels
15-20 prawns (*jheenga*), peeled and deveined
2 large pomfret fillets (125 grams each), cut into 1-inch pieces
Salt to taste
¾ cup yogurt (*dahi*), whisked
2 teaspoons ginger paste
2 teaspoons garlic paste
1 teaspoon green chilli paste
Oil for deep-frying
4 medium onions, sliced
2½ tablespoons pure *ghee*
1 bay leaf (*tej patta*)
6-8 black peppercorns (*kali mirch*)
2 black cardamoms (*badi elaichi*)
3-4 green cardamoms (*chhoti elaichi*)
1 star anise (*chakri phool /badiyan*)
2 inches cinnamon (*dalchini*)
½ teaspoon turmeric (*haldi*) powder
1¼ teaspoons red chilli powder
2 teaspoons garam masala powder
1 tablespoon coriander (*dhania*) powder
1 tablespoon lemon juice
2 tablespoons chopped fresh coriander (*hara dhania*)
10-12 fresh mint leaves (*pudina*), roughly torn

Method

1. Soak the rice in three cups of water for half an hour. Drain and set aside.
2. Wash the mussels and cook in boiling salted water for two minutes. Drain and set aside unshelled. Reserve the water.
3. Place the yogurt in a bowl; add half the ginger paste, half the garlic paste, half the green chilli paste and salt to taste and mix well. Add the prawns and pomfret and marinate for half an hour, preferably in a refrigerator.
4. Heat the oil in a *kadai* and deep-fry half the sliced onions till brown and crisp. Drain on absorbent paper.
5. Heat the *ghee* in a separate pan and add the bay leaf, peppercorns, black cardamoms, green cardamoms, star anise, cinnamon and the remaining sliced onions. Sauté for two minutes.
6. Add the remaining ginger, garlic and green chilli pastes. Stir well and add the rice. Sauté for two minutes and add the water in which the mussels were boiled. Add the turmeric powder, chilli powder, *garam masala* powder, coriander powder and saffron and mix well.
7. Add the marinated prawns and fish and the boiled mussels. Add the salt, lemon juice, chopped coriander and mint. Stir and add the fried onions.
8. Cover the pan and cook over a low heat for ten minutes. Remove from heat and leave to stand, covered, for five to ten minutes. Serve directly from the pan to retain maximum flavour.

MUSHROOM POT RICE

Serve steaming hot, with delicious aromas wafting out from under the lid...

Ingredients

3-4 oyster mushrooms
10-12 fresh button mushrooms, sliced
1 cup rice, soaked
1 star anise (*chakri phool/badiyan*)
2 tablespoons cornflour
4 tablespoons oil
1 inch ginger, grated
2-3 garlic cloves, chopped
2 spring onions, chopped
2 tablespoons soy sauce
¼ teaspoon MSG (optional)
½ teaspoon white pepper powder
2 cups Vegetable Stock (page 98)

Method

1. Boil the rice in three cups of water with the star anise until just cooked. Drain well, transfer to a clay pot and keep warm.
2. Soak the oyster mushrooms in hot water for fifteen minutes, drain and chop roughly. Mix the cornflour and half a cup of water. Set aside.
3. Preheat the oven to 180°C/350°F/Gas Mark 4.
4. Heat the oil in a wok; add the ginger and garlic and stir-fry for half a minute. Reserve some spring onions for garnishing, add the rest to the wok and continue to stir-fry for a minute.
5. Add the soy sauce, oyster mushrooms, MSG, white pepper powder and vegetable stock. Bring to a boil, add the button mushrooms and stir in the cornflour mixture.
6. Cook for a minute or until the sauce thickens, stirring continuously. Pour the sauce over the rice, cover with a lid and cook in the preheated oven for twelve to fifteen minutes.
7. Uncover the pot, stir the contents well, garnish with the reserved spring onion greens and serve hot.

RISOTTO PRIMAVERA

Serve this whenever you feel the family needs a treat with some great TV viewing.

Ingredients

2 cups arborio (risotto) rice
2 medium green capsicums (*hari Shimla mirch*)
6-8 fresh button mushrooms, sliced
4 medium carrots, sliced
2-3 fresh asparagus (*shatavari*) spears, cut into 1-inch pieces
4 tablespoons butter
1 medium onion, chopped
8 cups water or Vegetable Stock (page 98)
Salt to taste
½ cup grated Parmesan cheese
½ cup fresh cream
½ teaspoon white pepper powder

Method

1. Roast the capsicums over an open flame till the outer skin chars. Peel and quarter. Set aside.
2. Melt two tablespoons of butter in a deep pan over a low heat; add the onion and sauté until translucent.
3. Add the rice and sauté for one or two minutes. Add two cups of stock and salt and cook, stirring occasionally, till all the stock is absorbed.
4. Add the mushrooms, carrots and asparagus and mix well. Add the remaining stock and cook, stirring occasionally, for about twenty-five minutes, or till the rice is completely cooked.
5. Add the remaining butter, half the Parmesan cheese and the cream and mix well. Add the white pepper powder and mix well.
6. Add the roasted capsicums and serve hot, topped with the remaining Parmesan cheese.

SAOJI MUTTON

Spicy, succulent mutton curry with steaming hot rice. Simply wonderful and filling...

Ingredients

800 grams mutton on the bone, cut into 2-inch pieces
6 tablespoons oil
6 medium onions, sliced
2 tablespoons coriander seeds (*dhania*)
1 teaspoon caraway seeds (*shahi jeera*)
4-6 cloves (*laung*)
20 black peppercorns (*kali mirch*)
3-4 green cardamoms (*chhoti elaichi*)
4-5 black cardamoms (*badi elaichi*)
2 one-inch sticks cinnamon (*dalchini*)
4-5 bay leaves (*tej patta*)
8-10 dried red chillies
1 tablespoon poppy seeds (*khuskhus*)
½ cup sliced dried coconut (*khopra*)
1 tablespoon stone flower (*dagad phool*)
1 tablespoon ginger paste
1 tablespoon garlic paste
Salt to taste

Method

1. Heat four tablespoons of oil in a pan; add the onions, coriander seeds, caraway seeds, cloves, peppercorns, green and black cardamoms, cinnamon, bay leaves, red chillies, poppy seeds, dried coconut and stone flower and sauté over a low heat till fragrant. Cool and grind to a paste with a little water.
2. Heat the remaining oil in a pressure cooker. Add the ginger paste and garlic paste and sauté over a moderate heat for two minutes. Add the ground paste and sauté for one minute. Add the mutton and mix well. Add three cups of water and salt and bring the mixture to a boil.
3. Seal the cooker with the lid and cook till the pressure is released six or seven times (six or seven whistles).
4. Serve hot with steamed rice, *pav* or *chapati*.

VANILLA SPONGE WITH FRUIT CREAM

Cake 'n' cream and a soppy movie...the perfect match!

Ingredients

1 eight-inch round sponge cake
1½ cups whipped cream
2 medium plums, stoned and quartered
2 medium peaches, stoned, peeled and quartered
6-8 cherries, stoned

Method

1. Slice the cake horizontally into two.
2. Spread the whipped cream on both the halves.
3. Arrange the plums, peaches and cherries over the cream in an attractive pattern.
4. Cut into wedges and serve immediately.

STICKY DATE PUDDING

As sinful as brownies with cream, but a healthier version of a favourite dessert.

Ingredients

1 cup refined flour (*maida*), sifted
1 cup pitted and chopped dates (*khajur*)
90 grams butter
½ teaspoon soda bicarbonate
½ cup soft brown sugar
2 eggs
1 teaspoon vanilla essence

Sauce

1 cup soft brown sugar
1 cup cream
90 grams butter
½ teaspoon vanilla essence

Method

1. Preheat the oven to 180°C/350°F/Gas Mark 4.
2. Brush a deep seven-inch square cake tin with melted butter and line the base with butter paper.
3. Place the dates and soda bicarbonate in a heatproof bowl and add one cup of boiling water. Stir and leave for fifteen minutes to soften.
4. Using an electric beater, beat the butter and brown sugar until light and creamy. Beat in the eggs gradually. Add the vanilla essence.
5. Fold in half the sifted flour, then half the date mixture. Stir in the remaining flour and dates and mix well.
6. Pour the mixture into the prepared tin and bake for fifty minutes or till a skewer inserted into the pudding comes out clean.
7. Leave the pudding in the tin to cool for ten minutes before turning out.
8. To make the sauce, place the sugar, cream, butter and vanilla essence in a pan and bring to a boil, stirring continuously. Lower the heat and simmer for five minutes.
9. Serve the warm pudding with the hot sauce.

Green Chutney

Grind together 1 cup fresh coriander, ½ cup fresh mint, 2-3 green chillies, black salt to taste, ¼ teaspoon sugar and 1 tablespoon lemon juice to a smooth paste using a little water if required.

Thousand Island Dressing

Mix together ¾ cup Mayonnaise (page 99), 1 tablespoon tomato ketchup, 1 teaspoon Tabasco sauce, 3-4 chopped, stoned olives, 2-3 chopped pickled onions and 2 chopped pickled gherkins.

Chicken Stock

Boil 200 grams chicken bones in water for 5 minutes. Drain and discard water. Boil blanched bones with a roughly chopped carrot, celery stalk, leek, 2-3 parsley stalks, 6-7 black peppercorns, 5-6 cloves, 1 bay leaf and 10 cups of water.
Remove any scum which rises to the surface and replace it with more cold water.
Simmer for at least one hour.
Remove from heat, strain, cool and store in a refrigerator till further use.

Vegetable Stock

Peel, wash and chop 1 onion, ½ medium carrot, 2-3 inch celery stalk and 2-3 garlic cloves. Place in a pan with 1 bay leaf, 5-6 black peppercorns, 2-3 cloves and five cups of water and bring to a boil. Lower heat and simmer for fifteen minutes and strain. Cool and store in a refrigerator till further use.

MAYONNAISE

Ingredients

1 egg yolk
Salt to taste
¼ teaspoon white pepper powder
¼ teaspoon French mustard
¼ teaspoon sugar
1 teaspoon vinegar (*sirka*)
1 cup oil
1 teaspoon lemon juice

Method

1. Place the egg yolk, salt, white pepper powder, mustard, sugar and vinegar in a clean bowl and mix thoroughly with a whisk. Alternatively, process the mixture in a blender.
2. Add the oil, a little at a time, whisking or blending continuously, until all the oil is incorporated.
3. Add the lemon juice and adjust seasoning.
4. Store in an airtight jar in the refrigerator.

WHITE SAUCE

Ingredients

1½ tablespoons refined flour (*maida*)
2 tablespoons butter
1 medium onion
1 bay leaf (*tej patta*)
2 cloves (*laung*)
1½ cups milk
A small pinch of grated nutmeg (*jaiphal*)
Salt to taste
¼ teaspoon white pepper powder

Method

1. Melt one and a half tablespoons of butter in a thick-bottomed pan.
2. Add the flour; stir and cook the roux (butter-flour mixture) over a low heat with a wooden spoon. When it develops a sandy texture, remove from heat and cool.
3. Peel the onion. Wrap a bay leaf around it, studding it with cloves at the two ends.
4. Add the onion to the milk and bring to boil. Remove the onion, and pour the boiling hot milk into the cold roux, stirring continuously, to prevent lumps from forming. Simmer gently for two minutes. Add the nutmeg, salt and white pepper powder.
5. Melt the remaining butter and gently pour over the top of the sauce to prevent a skin forming.

Makes 1½ cups

Books by Master Chef Sanjeev Kapoor

Small Format

Title	MRP ₹
The Party Food Cookbook	110
Non-Vegetarian Soups and Salads	99
Best of Paneer: A collection of Vegetarian Recipes	99
Cocktail Snacks	99
Desi Murgh	99
Curries	99
South Indian Snacks	99
Roti-Paranthe	110
Vegetarian Breakfast Bonanza	125
Scrumptious Vegetarian Salads	99
Delicious Vegetarian Soups	99
Vegetarian After-School Snacks	125
Vegetarian Soups	125
Recipes for Non-Stick Cookware	125
Vegetarian Cooking with Dahi	110
Go Green	99
Healthy Tasty Recipes	99
Monsoon Medley	99
Chill Out! Summer Eats and Treats	99
Mango Masti	99
Tawa-Handi Recipes	125
Sunday Specials	125
Simple Home Baking	110
Chai-Nashta	125
Mirch Mazaa	125
Sweet Temptations	110
Dal-Roti	99
Desi Sabziyan	110
Pickles, Chutneys 'n' More	110
Say Cheese!	99
Mushroom Mania	99
Noodles and Pasta	110
Makai Magic	99
Eggs	99
Desi Aloo	99
Dahi	125
Rice, Biryani and Pulao	125
Vegetarian Rice, Biryani and Pulao	125
Kadai Cooking	110
Pressure Cooking	99
No-Oil Recipes	99
No-Oil Vegetarian Recipes	110
Street Food	125
Desi Mutton	95
Thai Cooking	99
Paneer	110
Italian Cooking	99
Drinks and Mocktails	125
Vegetarian Breakfasts	125
Salads	125
Non-Vegetarian Recipes from Around the World	99
Vegetarian Recipes from Around the World	110
Seafood	125
Chicken Recipes	125
Punjabi	99
Chinese Non-Vegetarian Cooking	110
Chinese Vegetarian Cooking	99
Microwave Desi Cooking	110
Sweet Encounters	99
Soups, Salads and Sandwiches	110
Vegetarian Snacks and Starters	110
Non-Vegetarian Snacks and Starters	110

Big Format

Title	MRP ₹
The Yellow Chilli Cookbook	595
Mithai - Sweets for Every Celebration	295
Kitchen Library Eat Lite - Low-Calorie Vegetarian Collection (set of 5 volumes)	485
Cooking with Love - Vegetarian Recipes from My Mother's Kitchen	295
Healthy Indian Cooking for Diabetes	345
100 Favourite Hand-Picked Recipes	595
Fun Food for Fussy Kids	350
Kitchen Library Vegetarian Collection (set of 5 volumes)	485
Simply Stylish - Entertaining at Home	395
Wedding Collection - Recipes for Newly-Weds	1200
Dakshin Delights	295
Everyday Indian with Olive Oil	495
Marwari Vegetarian Cooking	295
Tandoori Cooking @ Home	275
Flavours of the Orient	250
Wrap 'N' Roll	350
Party Cooking	295
Dal and Kadhi	350
Chaat	350
T.V. Dinner	350
Cakes and Bakes	295
No-Oil Vegetarian Cooking	275
No-Oil Cooking	295
Konkan Cookbook	275
Simply Indian	275
Royal Hyderabadi Cooking	350
Best of Chinese Cooking	275
Microwave Cooking Made Easy	295
Khazana of Healthy Tasty Recipes	250
Any Time Temptations	295
Low Calorie Vegetarian Cookbook	295
Khana Khazana: Celebration of Indian Cookery	295
Khazana of Indian Vegetarian Recipes	275
Khazana of Indian Recipes	295

NEW RELEASES

Big Format

Title	MRP ₹
Everyday Cooking	295
Aah! Chocolate	595
Low-Salt Cookbook	195
Tiffins - Delicious and Healthy Khana for Dabba	295

Small Format

Title	MRP ₹
Iron-Rich Recipes	110
Vegetarian Finger Foods	110
Kabab Lajawab!	99
Vegetarian Recipes from Marwar	99
Noodles and Rice	99

Buy online from www.sanjeevkapoor.com